CHRISTIAN WEDDINGS

Resources to Make Your Ceremony Unique

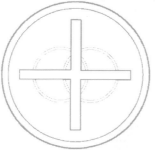

ANDY LANGFORD

ABINGDON PRESS / *Nashville*

CHRISTIAN WEDDINGS

You may order a software edition of this book from your religious bookstore or by calling 1-800-672-1789.

97 98 99 00 01 02 03 04 05 — 10 9 8 7 6 5 4

CONTENTS

❧ 1. HOW TO MAKE YOUR WEDDING UNIQUE

This book is for you, if you are:

- ❧ a couple desiring a unique, personalized service
- ❧ a pastor desiring wedding resources from a variety of worship traditions
- ❧ a couple planning your own wedding
- ❧ a pastor assisting a couple in planning their wedding
- ❧ a couple coming from different worship traditions, such as a United Methodist bride marrying a Presbyterian groom.

This book is a collection of the finest available Christian marriage resources from the major Christian worship traditions throughout the English-speaking world. It provides resources for Christian marriage for couples who wish to sanctify their marriage in a service of Christian worship. These resources testify that this is a Christian marriage, while encouraging each individual couple to make their personal witness. To make a service more specific to an individual couple, each couple has the freedom to amend these resources to reflect their commitments in the marriage covenant. For couples who are not church members or are not prepared to make the Christian commitment expressed in these resources, the couple and pastor may make adaptations. Each marriage service should reflect the values and beliefs that the couple share. The primary purpose of your service is to make marriage a joyful celebration of the presence of God.

Marriage services in the present day demand such a rich collection. Half of Catholics intermarry, 69 percent of Methodists marry non-Methodists, 70 percent of Lutherans marry non-Lutherans, 75 percent of Presbyterians marry non-Presbyterians. "Intermarriage today is the American way: bonds of love take precedence over bonds of faith, bonds of ethnicity, and occasionally even bonds of color" (Jonathan Sarna, *Commentary*, October 1994).

The words and actions in each of these resources consistently reflect the belief that husband and wife are equal partners in Christian marriage and that they are entering into the marriage of their own free-will.

A minister, pastor, or priest (labeled throughout this book as "pastor") normally presides at a service of Christian marriage. The decision to perform the ceremony is the right and responsibility of the pastor, in accordance with the laws of the state and the particular denomination. In addition to premarital counseling, each pastor should plan the marriage service with both members of the couple.

At this time, the pastor should also inform the couple of policies or guidelines established by the congregation on such matters as decorations, photography, and audio or video recording. Any other clergy and laity involved as leaders of this worship service should be invited by the pastor of the church where the service is held. Any pastor who is mediating a wedding and using this book with a couple is very likely a flexible and supportive servant of the Church. Pastors want couples to experience and remember their day of covenant as original and unique—in fact so unique that it need not happen again! The pastor is available to serve, and thus should approve the final plans for the wedding service in negotiation with the couple.

The guests at a wedding should be an active congregation rather than simply passive witnesses or spectators. These resources encourage the congregation to give their blessing to the couple and their marriage, and join in prayer and praise. It is highly appropriate that the congregation sing hymns and participate through other acts of worship. A worship bulletin is vital if you wish the guests to participate fully in the service.

Any children of the man or the woman, other family members, and friends may take a variety of roles in the service, depending on their ages and abilities. They may, for example, be members of the wedding party, participate in the Response of the Families and Children, read Scripture lessons, sing or play instrumental music, or make a witness in their own words. As families become more diverse, carefully involve as many members of the families as possible.

The person who makes the music possible, such as an organist or pianist, should be consulted and work with the couple in all decisions on music selection. The wedding hymns listed in this book are a starting place for choosing congregational music. No aspect of the service is more important than music, because the music dramatically affects the mood of the service, and the mood is what most couples recall. The couple and music director can carefully choose all the music to reflect the tastes of the couple and to witness to the Christian nature of the service. Music may be incorporated at many places throughout the traditional service. By working together, the pastor and musician can easily design a unified service.

A wedding director is helpful as a facilitator during a wedding, but the director is not the designer of the service itself. The director should have a copy of the service you design, and then guide all the participants through the service. It is especially helpful if the director has a copy of the service before the rehearsal, but given the sacred aspects of a Christian wedding, it should be the pastor who directs the service during rehearsal.

This resource does not include details about the many other arrangements that may be necessary for a wedding: such as flowers, banners, a wedding reception, rehearsal dinner/party, and the other items that establish an environment for celebration. A number of other fine resources will assist the couple in making these plans. Be mindful, however, that the amount and cost of the "extras" at a marriage service should reflect the religious values of the couple rather than our expectations as consumers. Most couples feel the strong temptation to be extravagant, to make a statement. The heart of the marriage service should be, however, the covenant ceremony itself, rather than the flowers, candles, and reception.

Ethnic and cultural traditions are encouraged and may be incorporated into the service. For example, Hispanic couples have a tradition of the couple wearing a large loop of rosary beads. The loop is placed in a figure-eight shape around the necks of the man and woman after they say their vows.

A church sanctuary, or outside in a garden, a mountaintop, or other setting are all highly appropriate for Christian weddings. While many couples continue to be married in the bride's home congregation, increasingly couples choose a location most convenient or memorable for all members of the wedding party. Wherever the wedding takes place, the couple should be alert that the setting not detract from the Christian character of the service itself.

The basic outline of a Christian wedding is held in common by most churches, and this book follows this outline (see the Contents, p. 3). Whenever the couple or pastor deems that changes are appropriate, however, it is possible to change this basic outline.

The resources in this book include the major current services of Christian Marriage of churches around the world. While not every word of every service is included, this book includes the most distinctive contributions of each tradition. The book includes abbreviated names, which reflect the resources used. They are:

African Methodist Episcopal is The Solemnization of Matrimony I of the *African Methodist Episcopal Church Book of Worship*. It was published in 1984 by this predominately African-African denomination.

Alternatives comes from *Wedding Alternatives*, a 1990s resource of socially responsible wedding resources and ideas, published by the nondenominational organization, Alternatives.

Australian is the Marriage Service of The Uniting Church in Australia, found in the 1988 book, *Uniting in Worship*. This is the dominant Protestant church in Australia. The spelling of words has been changed to conform to usage in the United States.

Baptist are resources from Baptist congregations throughout the United States, found in *The Wedding Collection* by Morris H. Chapman and published in 1991 by Broadman Press. Some changes are made to make the language more inclusive.

British Methodist is the Marriage Service of the 1975 *Methodist Service Book* of the British Methodist Conference. It is a contemporary updating of services unique to the Wesleyan tradition.

Canadian Anglican is the Marriage Service of *The Book of Alternative Services* of the Anglican Church of Canada published in 1985. This is an alternative service book to the traditional Anglican *Book of Common Prayer*.

Church of England is the Marriage Service of *The Alternative Service Book for use in the Church of England in conjunction with The Book of Common Prayer*, published in 1980. It is a contemporary updating of the classic *Book of Common Prayer*. The spelling of words has been changed to conform to usage in the United States.

Church of Scotland is The First Order for the Celebration of Marriage from *The Book of Common Order* of 1979 of the Church of Scotland.

Church of South India is the Marriage Service from the Church of South India of 1962 as found in The Book of Common Worship of *The Church of South India*. This was one of the first contemporary worship books.

Episcopal, from 1979, is a Celebration and Blessing of a Marriage from *The Book of Common Prayer* according to the use by The Episcopal Church in the United States. This service is the basis of many wedding resources throughout the United States.

Evangelical Covenant is the Rite of Marriage II from *The Covenant Book of Worship* of The Evangelical Covenant Church of America, published in 1981.

Evangelical United Brethren is a traditional text from the ritual of the Evangelical United Brethren Church found in *The Book of Ritual of The Evangelical United Brethren Church*, published in 1959. This church was one of the predecessors of The United Methodist Church.

Lutheran is the Marriage text from 1978 found in *The Lutheran Book of Worship* of the Lutheran Church, U.S.A., The Evangelical Lutheran Church of Canada, and The Lutheran Church—Missouri Synod.

Methodist is a traditional United Methodist marriage service, based primarily on the 1965 service from the *Methodist Book of Worship for Church and Home*, with additions from the 1959 Evangelical United Brethren *Book of Ritual*. This service is also found in *The United Methodist Book of Worship* (1992). This church was one of the predecessors of The United Methodist Church.

Moravian is the 1995 Wedding Service of the Moravian Church, found in the *Book of Worship*.

Presbyterian is the 1993 Christian Marriage from the *Book of Common Worship* of the Presbyterian Church (U.S.A.) and the Cumberland Presbyterian Church.

Reformed Church is the 1987 Order of Worship for Christian Marriage of the Reformed Church in America, found in *Worship the Lord*.

Roman Catholic comes from The Wedding Mass of *The Sacramentary* approved for use in the Dioceses of the United States of America by the National Conference of Catholic Bishops and confirmed by the Apostolic See. This book was published by The Liturgical Press in 1985.

United Church of Canada is the 1985 Rite II Wedding Service of the *Common Order of the United Church of Canada*. This church is the dominant Protestant denomination in Canada.

United Church of Christ is a 1986 Service of Marriage from the *Book of Worship of The United Church of Christ*, a contemporary service stressing the equality of the man and woman.

United Methodist is a contemporary Service of Christian Marriage found in *The United Methodist Book of Worship*, published in 1992. This service is also found in the 1989 *United Methodist Hymnal*.

WEDDING WORKSHEET

*A*s you read this book, fill out the following worksheet. List the number of each resource you wish to use. You are not required to choose an item under each category. Select only the resources that you wish to incorporate into your own unique service. At the end of this process, you will have planned a Christian wedding.

These resources are also found in *Christian Weddings: Software Edition*. Pastors and others will be able to "cut and paste" the resources chosen into a customized service, and then can print a copy from a word processor.

You may order the software version by calling 1-800-672-1789, or from your local bookstore. Specify whether your system is a Macintosh (order #017033), or running Windows (order #014557).

COUPLE:

How the couple is to be addressed during wedding:

Date and time of wedding:

Place of wedding:

	First Choice	Second Choice
2. GATHERING		
3. GREETING		
4. CHARGE TO THE MAN AND WOMAN		
5. DECLARATION OF INTENTION/CONSENT		
6. PRESENTATION	Daniel	
7. RESPONSE OF FAMILIES		
RESPONSE OF CHILDREN		
RESPONSE OF CONGREGATION		
8. OPENING PRAYER		
9. SCRIPTURE LESSONS		
HYMNS		

	First Choice	Second Choice
PSALMS		
10. INTERCESSORY PRAYER	Father Tom	
11. EXCHANGE OF VOWS		
12a. TAKING OF RINGS		
12b. BLESSING OF RINGS		
12c. EXCHANGING OF RINGS		
13. UNITY CANDLE		
14. DECLARATION OF MARRIAGE		
15. BLESSING OF THE MARRIAGE	Father Tom	
16. THE LORD'S PRAYER		
17. THANKSGIVING AND COMMUNION		
PRAYER AFTER COMMUNION		
18. DISMISSAL WITH BLESSING		
SPECIAL MUSIC		

Prayer for dinner

❦ 2. GATHERING

While the people gather, instrumental or vocal music may be offered on musical instruments, by singers, or on tape. Church bells may be rung. Here and throughout the service, while the use of music appropriate for Christian worship is strongly encouraged, all decisions finally rest in the hands of the couple and pastor.

During the Gathering, guests and families are seated and candles lighted.

During the entrance of the wedding party, there may be a hymn, a psalm, a canticle (a song from Scripture), or an anthem. The congregation may be invited to stand. The following processional hymns may be found in a variety of hymnals:

> All Creatures of Our God and King
> All Praise to Thee, for Thou, O King Divine
> Amazing Grace
> Blest Are They
> Christ Is Made the Sure Foundation
> Come Down, O Love Divine
> Come, My Way, My Truth, My Life
> Come, Thou Almighty King
> Come, We That Love the Lord
> For the Beauty of the Earth
> God of Our Life
> Hear Us Now, Our God
> How We Name a Love

In Thee Is Gladness
Jesus, Joy of Our Desiring
Joyful, Joyful We Adore Thee
Let All the World in Every Corner Sing
Let's Sing Unto the Lord/ Cantemos al Senor
Lord of All Hopefulness
Love Divine, All Loves Excelling
O God, Our Help in Ages Past
O Perfect Love
O Young and Fearless Prophet
Praise, My Soul, the King of Heaven
Praise the Lord Who Reigns Above
Praise to the Lord, the Almighty
Sing Praise to God Who Reigns Above
The King of Lord My Shepherd Is
Where Charity and Love Prevail
Where Love Is Found
Ye Watchers and Ye Holy Ones
Your Love, O God, Has Called Us Here

The wedding party enters at this time. Typically, this is the order followed: the groom's grandparents, the bride's grandparents, the groom's parents, the bride's mother. The wedding party follows, including ushers, bridesmaids, maid (unmarried woman)/ matron (married woman) of honor, ring bearer, and flower girl(s).

The woman and the man, entering separately or together, now come forward with members of the wedding party. The woman and the man may be escorted by representatives of their families (traditionally, the groom by his father or best man, and the bride by her father or other male family member) until they have reached the front of the church, or through the Response of the Families, at which time their escorts are seated. The couple may also enter separately and alone, or together. The way the couple enters says much about their relationship to one another, and their relationship to their family members. Plan carefully the entrance of the bride and groom.

❦ 3. GREETING

The Greeting, an invitation to worship by the pastor facing the people, introduces the couple and the congregation to the nature of Christian marriage and welcomes the congregation. This time often includes the biblical witness about marriage, such as Jesus' participation in the wedding at Cana of Galilee. A short prayer or reading from Scripture may preface the Greeting. According to the tradition of the Church of South India, the man and woman place garlands of flowers on each other following the Greeting.

3.1

Friends, we are gathered together in the sight of God
to witness and bless the joining together of *Name* and *Name*
    in Christian marriage.
The covenant of marriage was established by God,
    who created us male and female for each other.
With his presence and power
    Jesus graced a wedding at Cana of Galilee,
and in his sacrificial love
    gave us the example for the love of husband and wife.
Name and *Name* come to give themselves to one another
    in this holy covenant.   (United Methodist)

3.2

Dearly beloved,
we are gathered together here in the sight of God,
    and in the presence of these witnesses,
        to join together this man and this woman (*Name* and *Name*)
    in holy matrimony,

which is an honorable estate, instituted of God,
    and signifying unto us
        the mystical union that exists
        between Christ and his Church;
which holy estate Christ adorned and beautified
    with his presence in Cana of Galilee.
It is therefore not to be entered into unadvisedly,
    but reverently, discreetly, and in the fear of God.
Into this holy estate these two persons come now to be joined.

                                     (Methodist)

3.3

The grace of our Lord Jesus Christ, the love of God,
    and the communion of the Holy Spirit be with you all.

And also with you.

Let us pray.
Eternal God, our creator and redeemer,
    as you gladdened the wedding at Cana in Galilee
    by the presence of your Son,
so by his presence now bring your joy to this wedding.
Look in favor upon *Name* and *Name*
    and grant that they, rejoicing in all your gifts,
    may at length celebrate with Christ
    the marriage feast which has no end.
Amen.   (Lutheran)

3.4

Dearly beloved:
We have come together in the presence of God to witness and bless

the joining together of this man and this woman
in Holy Matrimony.
The bond and covenant of marriage
was established by God in creation,
and our Lord Jesus Christ adorned this manner of life
by his presence and first miracle
at a wedding in Cana of Galilee.
It signifies to us the mystery of the union
between Christ and his Church,
and Holy Scripture commends it
to be honored among all people.
The union of husband and wife in heart, body, and mind
is intended by God for their mutual joy;
for the help and comfort given one another
in prosperity and adversity;
and when it is God's will, for the procreation of children
and their nurture in the knowledge and love of the Lord.
Therefore marriage is not to be entered into
unadvisedly or lightly,
but reverently, deliberately,
and in accordance with the purposes
for which it was instituted by God.   (Episcopalian)

3.5

Love comes from God.
Everyone who truly loves is a child of God.
Let us worship God.   (United Church of Christ)

3.6

Dearly beloved, we are gathered here as the people of God
to witness the marriage of *Name* and *Name*.

We come to share in their joy and to ask God to bless them.
Marriage is a gift of God, sealed by a sacred covenant.
God gives human love.
Through that love, husband and wife
    come to know each other with mutual care and companionship.
God gives joy.
Through that joy,
    wife and husband may share their new life with others
    as Jesus shared new wine at the wedding in Cana.
With our love and our prayers,
    we support *Name* and *Name*
    as they now freely give themselves to each other.

(United Church of Christ)

3.7

Dear friends, we have come together in the presence of God
    to witness the marriage of *Name* and *Name*,
    to surround them with our prayers, and to share in their joy.
The scriptures teach us
    that the bond and covenant of marriage is a gift of God,
    a holy mystery in which man and woman become one flesh,
    an image of the union of Christ and the church.
As this woman and this man give themselves to each other today,
    we remember that at Cana in Galilee
    our Savior Jesus Christ made the wedding feast
    a sign of God's reign of love.
Let us enter into this celebration
    confident that through the Holy Spirit,
Christ is present with us now.
We pray that this couple may fulfill God's purpose
    for the whole of their lives.   (United Church of Christ)

3.8

God is love, and those who abide in love,
  abide in God, and God abides in them.   1 John 4:16

This is the day that the Lord has made;
  let us rejoice and be glad in it.   Psalm 118:24

O give thanks, for the Lord is good.
God's love endures forever.   Psalm 106:1   (Presbyterian)

3.9

We gather in the presence of God
  to give thanks for the gift of marriage,
  to witness the joining together of *Name* and *Name*,
  to surround them with our prayers,
and to ask God's blessing upon them,
  so that they may be strengthened for their life together
and nurtured in their love for God.
God created us male and female, and gave us marriage
  so that husband and wife may help and comfort each other,
  living faithfully together in plenty and in want,
  in joy and in sorrow, in sickness and in health,
  throughout all their days.
God gave us marriage
  for the full expression of the love
  between a man and a woman.
In marriage a woman and a man belong to each other,
  and with affection and tenderness
  freely give themselves to each other.
God gave us marriage for the well-being of human society,
  for the ordering of family life,

23

and for the birth and nurture of children.
God gave us marriage as a holy mystery
   in which a man and a woman are joined together,
and become one, just as Christ is one with the church.
In marriage, husband and wife are called to a new way of life,
   created and ordered, and blessed by God.
This way of life must not be entered into carelessly,
   or from selfish motives, but responsibly, and prayerfully.
We rejoice that marriage is given by God,
   blessed by our Lord Jesus Christ,
   and sustained by the Holy Spirit.
Therefore, let marriage be held in honor by all.   (Presbyterian)

3.10

Marriage is appointed by God.
The church believes that marriage is a gift of God in creation
   and a means of grace in which man and woman
      become one in heart, mind, and body.
Marriage is the sacred and life-long union of a man and a woman
   who give themselves to each other in love and trust.
It signifies the mystery of the union
   between Christ and the church.
Marriage is given that husband and wife
   may enrich and encourage each other
   in every part of their life together.
Marriage is given that with delight and tenderness
   they may know each other in love,
and through their physical union
   may strengthen the union of their lives.
Marriage is given that children may be born
   and brought up in security and love,

that home and family life may be strengthened,
and that society may stand upon firm foundations.
Marriage is a way of life which all people should honor;
it is not to be entered into lightly or selfishly,
but responsibly and in the love of God.
Name and *Name* are now to begin this way of life
which God has created and Christ has blessed.
Therefore, on this their wedding day, we pray for them,
asking that they may fulfill God's purpose
for the whole of their lives.

(Australian)

3.11

Dearly beloved, we are gathered together here
in the sight of God and these witnesses,
to join together this man and this woman
in the holy estate of matrimony.
The Bible teaches that marriage was created by God.
God made a helpmate for Adam and called her woman,
for she was taken from the man.
In the Old Testament, Moses, the lawgiver,
gave divine sanction to marriage as a legal institution.
In the New Testament,
the Book of Hebrews says
that marriage is honorable among all.
Therefore, because God has put His blessing upon this union,
and this is a service of Christian worship
celebrating the work of God,
let us pause to ask
for God's blessing and presence in this service.

(Baptist)

3.12

Dear friends, we have come together in the presence of God
    to witness the marriage of *Name* and *Name*,
    and to rejoice with them.
Marriage is a gift of God and a means of His grace,
    in which man and woman become one flesh.
It is God's purpose that
    as husband and wife give themselves to each other in love,
    they shall grow together and be united in that love,
    as Christ is united with his Church.
The union of man and woman in heart, body, and mind
    is intended for their mutual comfort and help,
    that they may know each other
    with delight and tenderness in acts of love
(and that they may be blessed
    in the procreation, care, and upbringing of children).
In marriage, husband and wife give themselves to each other,
    to care for each other in good times and in bad.
They are linked to each other's families,
    and they begin a new life together in the community.
It is a way of life that all should reverence,
    and none should lightly undertake.   (Canadian Anglican)

3.13

Christian marriage is a joyful covenanting
    between a man and a woman
    in which they proclaim, before God and human witnesses,
    their commitment to live together
    in spiritual, physical, and material unity.
In this covenant
they acknowledge that the great love

God has shown for each of them
   enables them to love each other.
They affirm that God's gracious presence and abiding power
   are needed for them to keep their vows, to continue to
   live in love,
   and to be faithful servants of Christ in this world.
For human commitment is fragile and human love imperfect,
   but the promise of God is eternal
   and the love of God can bring our love to perfection.

(Reformed Church)

3.14

Unless the Lord builds the house,
   its builders will have toiled in vain.
Our help is in the Name of the Lord,
Maker of heaven and earth.

Beloved, we have come together in the house of God
   to celebrate the marriage of this man and this woman,
   in the assurance that the Lord Jesus Christ,
   whose power was revealed at the wedding in Cana of Galilee,
   is present with us here in all his power and his love.

Marriage is provided by God
   as part of God's loving purpose for humanity
   since the beginning of creation.
Jesus said,
   "The Creator made them from the beginning male and female.
For this reason a man shall leave his father and mother,
   and be made one with his wife:
and the two shall become one flesh."

Marriage is enriched by God for all who have faith in the Gospel,
    for through the saving grace of Christ
    and the renewal of the Holy Spirit
    husband and wife can love one another as Christ loves them.

Marriage is thus a gift and calling of God
    and is not to be undertaken lightly or from selfish motives
        but with reverence and dedication,
    with faith in the enabling power of Christ,
    and with due awareness of the purpose
    for which it is appointed by God.

Marriage is appointed that there may be lifelong companionship,
    comfort and joy between husband and wife.

It is appointed as the right and proper setting
    for the full expression of physical love
    between man and woman.

It is appointed for the ordering of family life,
    where children—who are also God's gifts to us—
    may enjoy the security of love and the heritage of faith.

It is appointed for the well-being of human society,
    which can be stable and happy only
where the marriage bond is honored and upheld.

                              (Church of Scotland)

3.15

I will sing of your steadfast love, O Lord, forever;
    with my mouth I will proclaim your faithfulness
    to all generations.

I declare that your steadfast love is established forever;
    your faithfulness is as firm as the heavens.

Psalm 89:1-2

3.16

Praise the Lord!
Praise the name of the Lord!
Give praise, O servants of the Lord,
    you that stand in the house of the Lord,
    in the courts of the house of our God!
Praise the Lord, for the Lord is good;
    sing to the Lord's name, for the Lord is gracious!

Psalm 135:1-3

✿ 4. CHARGE TO THE MAN AND WOMAN

The pastor addresses the couple who are to marry and asks publicly about their free and mutual decision to marry. The Charge typically reminds the couple about the serious nature of the marriage covenant. Check to be sure that the Charge complements the opening Greeting.

4.1

I ask you now, in the presence of God and these people,
to declare your intention
to enter into union with each other
through the grace of Jesus Christ,
    who calls you into union with himself
    as acknowledged in your baptism.   (United Methodist)

4.2

I require and charge you both,
    as you stand in the presence of God,
    before whom the secrets of all hearts are disclosed,
    that, having duly considered the holy covenant
        you are about to make,
    you do now declare before this company
        your pledge of faith,
        each to the other.
Be well assured that if these solemn vows are kept inviolate,
    as God's Word demands,

and if steadfastly you endeavor to do
   the will of your heavenly Father,
God will bless your marriage,
   will grant you fulfillment in it,
   and will establish your home in peace.   (Methodist)

4.3

I charge you both, as you stand in the presence of God,
   to remember that love and loyalty alone will avail
      as the foundation of a happy home.
If the solemn vows you are about to make are kept faithfully,
   and if steadfastly you endeavor to do
      the will of your heavenly Father,
your life will be full of joy,
   and the home you are establishing will abide in peace.
No other ties are more tender, no other vows more sacred
   than those you now assume.   (Evangelical United Brethren)

4.4

The Lord God in His goodness created us male and female,
   and by the gift of marriage founded human community
      in a joy that begins now
      and is brought to perfection in the life to come.
Because of sin, our age-old rebellion,
   the gladness of marriage can be overcast
and the gift of the family can become a burden.
But because God, who established marriage,
   continues still to bless it
   with his abundant and ever-present support,
we can be sustained in our weariness
   and have our joy restored.

Name and *Name*, if it is your intention to share with each other
    your joy and sorrows and all that the years will bring,
  with your promises bind yourselves to each other
    as husband and wife.   (Lutheran)

4.5

Before God and this congregation,
  I ask you to affirm your willingness
    to enter this covenant of marriage
    and to share all the joys and sorrows
    of this new relationship,
    whatever the future may hold.   (United Church of Christ)

4.6

Name and *Name*,
  your marriage is intended to join you for life
    in a relationship so intimate and personal
    that it will change your whole being.
God offers you the hope, and indeed the promise,
    of a love that is true and mature.   (Evangelical Covenant)

🌿 5. DECLARATION OF INTENTION/CONSENT

The pastor speaks to the woman and the man individually and asks about their desire to be married. The Declaration often includes the specific obligations of the man and woman to each other.

5.1

Name, will you have *Name* to be your husband/wife,
   to live together in holy marriage?
Will you love him/her, comfort him/her, honor and keep him/her,
   in sickness and in health,
and forsaking all others, be faithful to him/her
   as long as you both shall live?

Woman/man: **I will.**   (United Methodist)

5.2

Name, will you have this woman/man
   to be your wedded wife/husband,
   to live together in the holy estate of matrimony?
Will you love her/him, comfort her/him
   honor and keep her/him,
   in sickness and in health;
and forsaking all others keep only to her/him
   so long as you both shall live?
Man/woman: **I will.**   (Methodist)

5.3

> *Name*, will you have this man/woman to be your husband/wife;
>> to live together in the covenant of marriage?
>
> Will you love him/her, comfort him/her,
>> honor and keep him/her,
>>
>> in sickness and in health;
>
> and, forsaking all others,
>> be faithful to him/her as long you both shall live?

> *Man/woman:* **I will.**   (Episcopalian)

5.4

> *Name,* will you have *Name* to be your wife/husband,
>> and will you love her/him faithfully
>>
>> as long as you both shall live?

> *Man/woman:* **I will.**   (United Church of Christ)

5.5

> *Name,* understanding that God has created, ordered,
>> and blessed the covenant of marriage,
>
> do you affirm your desire and intention to enter this covenant?

> *Man/woman:* **I do.**   (Presbyterian)

5.6

> *If both are baptized, the following may be used in addition to
> the above:*

> *Name,* in your baptism
>> you have been called to union with Christ and the church.

Do you intend to honor this calling
through the covenant of marriage?

Man/woman: **I do.**   (Presbyterian)

5.7

Name, will you have this man/woman
to be your husband/wife?

Man/woman: **I will**.   (United Church of Canada)

5.8

Do you, *Name,* now take *Name*
to be your wife/husband;
and do you promise,
in the presence of God and before these witnesses,
to be a loving, faithful and loyal husband/wife to her/him,
until God shall separate you by death?

Man/woman: **I do.**   (Church of Scotland)

5.9

Name, will you have this woman/man, *Name,*
to be your wife/husband,
and cleave to her alone?

Man/woman: **I will.**   (Church of South India)

5.10

Name, do you take *Name* to be your wife/husband,
and do you commit yourself to her/him,

to be responsible in the marriage relationship,
to give yourself to her/him in love and work,
to invite her/him fully into your being
   so that she/he can know who you are,
to cherish her/him above all others
   and to respect her/his individuality,
     encouraging her/him to be herself/himself
and to grow in all that God intends?

Man/woman: **I do.**   (Evangelical Covenant)

❦ 6. PRESENTATION

If the woman is presented (not given!) in marriage, the pastor asks the presenter(s), traditionally the father of the bride, one of the following. Although this tradition comes out of the worldview that the woman is the property of her father, it is often now retained in a bride's first marriages as a sign of the families' blessing. This time may also include brief witnesses of love and support by the family, during which particular family traditions may remembered. During a subsequent marriage, the Presentation may be made by a child from a previous marriage.

6.1

If the woman is presented, the pastor asks the presenter(s):

Who presents this woman to be married to this man?

Presenter(s): **I (We) do.**   (United Methodist)

6.2

If the man is presented, the pastor asks the presenter(s):

Who presents this man to be married to this woman?

Presenter(s): **I (We) do.**   (United Methodist)

❦ 7. RESPONSE OF THE FAMILIES, CHILDREN, AND CONGREGATION

This response by families and/or congregation, declaring their affirmation of the marriage, may be in place of, or in addition to the Presentation above. This time may also include time for silent meditation (a Quaker tradition) or for members of the congregation to stand and to offer verbal support to the couple. Because of the diversity of families and congregations, be sure to include as many persons as possible.

7.1

Pastor to family members:

The marriage of *Name* and *Name* unites their families
    and creates a new one.
They ask for your blessing.

Parents and other representatives of the families may respond:

**We rejoice in your union,
and pray God's blessing upon you.**   (United Methodist)

7.2

Pastor to family members:

Do you who represent their families
rejoice in their union
and pray God's blessing upon them?
We do. (United Methodist)

7.3

Pastor to family members:

Will the families of *Name* and *Name*
 please stand/please answer
 in support of this couple.
Do you offer your prayerful blessing
 and loving support to this marriage?

Families: **I do.** (United Church of Christ)

7.4

*Children of the couple may repeat these or similar words,
prompted line by line, by the pastor:*

**We love both of you.
We bless your marriage.
Together we will be a family**. (United Methodist)

7.5

Pastor to children of the new family:

Name, you are entering a new family.

Will you give to this new family your trust, love, and affection?

Child: **I will, with the help of God.**

Pastor to bride and groom:

Name and *Name,* will you be faithful and loving parents
    to *Name* and *Name*?

Couple: **We will, with the help of God.**

(United Church of Christ)

7.6

Pastor to people:

Will all of you, by God's grace,
    do everything in your power
to uphold and care for these two persons in their marriage?

People: **We will.**   (United Methodist)

7.7

*The congregation repeats the following, prompted line by line,
by the pastor:*

**May you dwell in God's presence forever;
    may true and constant love preserve you.**   (Lutheran)

7.8

Pastor to people:

Will all of you witnessing these promises
   do all in your power
   to uphold these two persons in their marriage?

People: **We will.**   (Episcopalian)

7.9

Pastor to people:

Do you, as people of God,
   pledge your support and encouragement
   to the covenant commitment
   that *Name* and *Name* are making together?

People: **We do.**   (United Church of Christ)

7.10

Pastor to parents:

With gratitude for your love, support, and nurture through
      the years,
   this couple comes today to form a new family
   under God's blessing.
Do you grant to them the freedom to form a new family
   and seek God's blessing?
Do you grant them the freedom to form a new family
   and seek God's will?
Do you pledge to them your continuing love and support?

Do you promise to be quick to listen and slow to speak,
    and do you covenant to pray for them
        and the ministry God plans for them in the future?

Parents: **We do.**   (Baptist)

7.11

Pastor to families:

This couple needs the support of their families,
    for they cannot live out their vision alone.
Do you, their families,
    promise to continue to love and to nurture them,
    to keep your lives forever open to them,
that they, in turn, may love and nurture you?

Families: **We do.**   (Alternatives)

7.12

Pastor to congregation:

Do you promise to love and to nurture *Name* and *Name*,
    to be open to their friendship,
to support them and to be supported by them
    as they answer the calls of God in their marriage
    and in their ministries.

Congregation: **We do.**   (Alternatives)

❧ 8. OPENING PRAYER

The pastor or other worship leader offers a prayer to God, establishing that this wedding is a service of worship of God. The pastor may also include time for silent prayer for the couple or lead in a bidding prayer for the couple. These prayers often invite God's presence, give thanks for this wedding day, and bless the couple to be married.

8.1

God of all peoples,
>you are the true light illumining everyone.

You show us the way, the truth, and the life.

You love us even when we are disobedient.

You sustain us with your Holy Spirit.

We rejoice in your life in the midst of our lives.

We praise you for your presence with us,
>and especially in this act of solemn covenant;

through Jesus Christ our Lord. **Amen.**   (United Methodist)

8.2

O gracious and everliving God,
>you have created us male and female in your image:

Look mercifully upon this man and this woman
>who come to you seeking your blessing,

and assist them with your grace,

that with true fidelity and steadfast love
>they may honor and keep the promises and vows they make;

43

through Jesus Christ our Savior, who lives and reigns with you
in the unity of the Holy Spirit, one God, for ever and ever.
Amen. (Episcopalian)

8.3

O God, we gather to celebrate your gift of love
  and its presence among us.
We rejoice that two people have chosen to commit themselves
  to a life of loving faithfulness to one another.
We praise you, O God,
  for the ways you have touched our lives
  with a variety of loving relationships.
We give thanks that we have experienced your love
  through the life-giving love of Jesus Christ
  and through the care and affection of other people.
At the same time, we remember and confess to you, O God,
  that we often have failed to be loving,
  that we often have taken for granted
  the people for whom we care most.
We selfishly neglect and strain the bonds that unite us with others.
We hurt those who love us
  and withdraw from the community that encircles us.
Forgive us, O God.
Renew within us an affectionate spirit.
Enrich our lives with the gracious gift of your love
  so that we may embrace others with the same love.
May our participation in this celebration of love and commitment
  give to us a new joy
  and responsiveness to the relationship we cherish;
through Jesus Christ we pray. **Amen.**

Through the great depth and strength of God's love for us,
  God reaches out to us to forgive our sins and to restore us to life.
Be assured, children of God,
    that God's love enfolds us and upbuilds us
    so that we may continue to love one another
        as God has loved us.   (United Church of Christ)

8.4

Gracious God, always faithful in your love for us,
    we rejoice in your presence.
You create love. You unite us in one human family.
You offer your word and lead us in light.
You open your loving arms and embrace us with strength.
May the presence of Christ fill our hearts with new joy
    and make new the lives of your servants
    whose marriage we celebrate.
Bless all creation through this sign of your love
    shown in the love of *Name* and *Name* for each other.
May the power of your Holy Spirit
    sustain them and all of us in love that knows no end. **Amen.**
                                            (United Church of Christ)

8.5

God of our mothers and of our fathers,
    hear our pledges encouraging and supporting
    this union of *Name* and *Name*.
Bless us as we offer our prayerful and loving support
    to their marriage.
Bless them as they pledge their lives to each other.
With faith in you and in each other,
    may this couple always bear witness
    to the reality of the love to which we witness this day.

    May their love continue to grow,
        and may it be a true reflection of your love for us all;
    through Jesus Christ. **Amen.**   (United Church of Christ)

8.6

Gracious God, you are always faithful in your love for us.
Look mercifully upon *Name* and *Name*,
    who have come seeking your blessing.
Let your Holy Spirit rest upon them
    so that with steadfast love
        they may honor the promises they make this day,
through Jesus Christ our Savior. **Amen.**   (Presbyterian)

8.7

Father, when you created humankind
    you willed that man and wife should be one.
Bind *Name* and *Name* in the loving union of marriage
    and make their love fruitful
        so that they may be living witnesses
        to your divine love in the world.
We ask this through our Lord Jesus Christ, your Son,
    who lives and reigns with you and the Holy Spirit,
One God, for ever and ever.   (Roman Catholic)

8.8

Loving and beloved God,
    from the beginning you have made us
    to live in partnership with one another.
We pray for the presence of your Spirit with these two persons.
Fill their hearts with sincerity and truth
    as they enter this solemn covenant. **Amen.**
                (United Church of Canada)

❦ 9. SCRIPTURE LESSONS, HYMNS, AND PSALMS

One or more of the following Scripture lessons may be read by either the pastor or laypersons (such as members of the family or wedding party), as a witness to the Bible's affirmation of love and marriage. Other readings from popular literature or poetry may also be read. A hymn, psalm, canticle (a song from Scripture), anthem, or other music may be offered before or after the readings, during which the congregation may be invited to stand. If there are lengthy readings and/or a sermon, arrange for the wedding party to be seated at this time.

The lessons are listed in their order in the Bible.

9.1 Suggested Scripture Lessons

Genesis 1:26-28, 31a	The creation of man and woman
Genesis 2:4-10, 15-24	Becoming one flesh
Proverbs 3:3-6	A seal upon your heart
Song of Solomon 2:10-14, 16a; 8:6-7	Love is strong as death.
Isaiah 43:1-7	You are precious in God's eyes.
Isaiah 54:5-8	Your maker is your husband.
Isaiah 55:10-13	You shall go out in joy.
Isaiah 61:10–62:3	Rejoice in the Lord.
Isaiah 63:7-9	The steadfast love of the Lord

Jeremiah 31:31-34	New Covenant
Matthew 5:1-10, 13-16	The Beatitudes
Matthew 7:21, 24-27	A house built upon a rock
Matthew 19:3-6	One flesh
Matthew 22:35-40	Love, the greatest commandment
Mark 2:18-22	Joy in Christ as at a wedding
Mark 10:6-9, 13-16	No longer two but one
Mark 10:42-45	True greatness
John 2:1-11	The marriage feast at Cana
John 15:9-17	Remain in Christ's love.
Romans 12:1-2, 9-18	The life of a Christian
1 Corinthians 13	The greatest of these is love.
2 Corinthians 5:14-17	In Christ we are a new creation.
Ephesians 2:4-10	God's love for us
Ephesians 4:1-6	Called to the one hope
Ephesians 4:25-5:2	Members one of another
Philippians 2:1-2	The Christlike spirit
Philippians 4:4-9	Rejoice in the Lord.
Colossians 3:12-17	Live in love and thanksgiving.
1 John 3:18-24	Love one another.
1 John 4:7-16	God is love.
Revelation 19:1, 5-9a	The wedding feast of the Lamb

9.2 Suggested Hymns

As Man and Woman We Were Made
Be Thou My Vision
Come, Christians, Join to Sing
Come, My Way, My Truth, My Life
O Lord, May Church and Home Combine
O Perfect Love

The Gift of Love 40 8
The King of Love My Shepherd Is / 3 8
When Love Is Found 64 3
Where Charity and Love Prevail
Your Love, O God, Has Called Us Here

9.3 Suggested Psalms

8	Crowned with glory and honor
23	The Lord is my shepherd.
33	Rejoice in the Lord.
34	I will bless the Lord.
37	Trust in the Lord and do good.
67	May God be gracious to us.
100	Make a joyful noise to the Lord.
103	Bless the Lord, O my soul.
112	Happy are those who fear the Lord.
117	God's steadfast love
121	Lift up my eyes to the hills
145	The Lord is gracious.
148	Praise the Lord from the heavens.
150	Praise the Lord.

Following the Scripture lessons, psalm, and hymn, the pastor may preach a sermon to interpret the Scripture on marriage, or friends and family may speak briefly about marriage and/or the couple.

9.4 Prayer Before Scripture

Before the Scripture lessons, the following prayer may be said:

God of mercy,
>   your faithfulness to your covenant frees us to live together
>   in the security of your powerful love.
Amid the changing words of our generation,
>   speak your eternal Word that does not change.
Then may we respond to your gracious promises
>   by living in faith and obedience;
through our Lord Jesus Christ. **Amen.**   (Presbyterian)

❦ 10. INTERCESSORY PRAYER

Following the reading of Scripture, the pastor or everyone present may offer one of the following prayers for the couple.

10.1

Eternal God, Creator and Preserver of all life,
    Author of salvation, Giver of all grace:
Bless and sanctify with your Holy Spirit
    Name and *Name,* who come now to join in marriage.
Grant that they may give their vows to each other
    in the strength of your steadfast love.
Enable them to grow in love and peace
    with you and with one another all their days,
    that they may reach out
    in concern and service to the world;
    through Jesus Christ our Lord. **Amen.**   (United Methodist)

10.2

Eternal God, creator and preserver of all life,
    author of salvation, and giver of all grace:
Look with favor upon the world you have made,
    and for which your Son gave his life,
and especially upon this man and this woman
    whom you make one flesh in Holy Matrimony. **Amen.**

Give them wisdom and devotion
    in the ordering of their common life,
    that each may be to the other a strength in need,
a counselor in perplexity, a comfort in sorrow,
    and a companion in joy. **Amen.**

Grant that their wills be so knit together in your will,
    and their spirits in your Spirit,
        that they may grow in love and peace with you
        and one another all the days of their life. **Amen.**

Give them grace, when they hurt each other,
    to recognize and acknowledge their faults,
and to seek each other's forgiveness and yours. **Amen.**

Make their life together a sign of Christ's love
    to this sinful and broken world,
    that unity may overcome estrangement,
    forgiveness heal guilt, and joy conquer despair. **Amen.**

Bestow on them, if it is your will, the gift and heritage of children,
    and the grace to bring them up to know you,
to love you, and to serve you. **Amen.**

Give them such fulfillment of their mutual affection
    that they may reach out in love and concern for others.
Amen.

Grant that all married persons who have witnessed these vows
    may find their lives strengthened
    and their loyalties confirmed. **Amen.**

Grant that the bonds of our common humanity,
    by which all your children are united one to another,
and the living to the dead,
    may be so transformed by your grace,
    that your will may be done on earth as it is in heaven;
where, O Father, with your Son and the Holy Spirit,
you live and reign in perfect unity, now and for ever. **Amen.**

(Episcopalian)

10.3

Eternal God, without your grace no promise is sure.
Strengthen *Name* and *Name* with patience,
    kindness, gentleness,
    and all other gifts of your Spirit,
    so that they may fulfill the vows they have made.
Keep them faithful to each other and to you.
Fill them with such love and joy
    that they may build a home of peace and welcome.
Guide them by your Word to serve you all their days.
Help us all, O God,
    to do your will in each of our homes and lives.
Enrich us with your grace so that, supporting one another,
    we may serve those in need
and hasten the coming of peace, love, and justice on earth,
through Jesus Christ our Lord. **Amen.**   (Presbyterian)

10.4

Gracious God, your generous love surrounds us,
    and everything we enjoy comes from you.
In your great love you have given us the gift of marriage.
Bless *Name* and *Name* as they pledge their lives to each other;

that their love may continue to grow
   and be the true reflection of your love for us all;
through Jesus Christ our Lord. **Amen.**   (Australian)

10.5

Father, by your power you have made everything out of nothing.
In the beginning you created the universe
   and made humankind in your own likeness.
You gave man the constant help of woman
   so that man and woman should no longer be two, but one flesh,
      and you teach us
      that what you have united may never be divided.
Father, by your plan man and woman are united,
   and married life has been established
      as the one blessing that was not forfeited by original sin
   or washed away in the flood.
Look with love upon this woman, your daughter,
   now joined to her husband in marriage.
She asks your blessing.
Give her the grace of love and peace.
May she always follow the example of the holy women
   whose praises are sung in the scriptures.
May her husband put his trust in her
   and recognize that she is his equal
      and the heir with him to the life of grace.
May he always honor her and love her
   as Christ loves his bride, the Church.
Father, keep them always true to your commandments.
Keep them faithful in marriage
   and let them be living examples of Christian life.
Give them the strength which comes from the gospel

so that they may be witnesses of Christ to others.
(Bless them with children
    and help them to be good parents.
May they live to see their children's children.)
And, after a happy old age,
    grant them fullness of life within the kingdom of heaven.
We ask this through Christ our Lord.   (Roman Catholic)

10.6

Holy Father, you created humankind in your own image
    and made man and woman to be joined as husband and wife
in union of body and heart,
    and so fulfill their mission in this world.
Father, to reveal the plan of your love,
    you made the union of husband and wife
    an image of the covenant between you and your people.
In the fulfillment of this sacrament [sign],
    the marriage of Christian man and woman
        is a sign of the marriage between Christ and the Church.
Father, stretch out your hand, and bless *Name* and *Name*.
Lord, grant that as they begin to live this sacrament [sign]
    they may share with each other the gifts of your love
        and become one in heart and mind
    as witnesses to your presence in their marriage.
Help them to create a home together
    (and give them children to be formed by the gospel
        and to have a place in your family).
Give your blessings to *Name*, your daughter,
    so that she may be a good wife (and mother),
        caring for the home, faithful in love for her husband,
        generous and kind.

Give your blessings to *Name,* your son,
  so that he may be a faithful husband (and a good father).
Father, grant that as they come together to your table on earth,
  so they may one day
  have the joy of sharing your feast in heaven.
We ask this through Christ our Lord.   (Roman Catholic)

10.7

Holy Father, creator of the universe,
  maker of man and woman in your own likeness,
    source of blessing for married life,
  we humbly pray to you for this woman
    who today is united with her husband
    in this sacrament [sign] of marriage.
May your fullest blessing come upon her and her husband
  so that they may together rejoice in your gift of married love
    (and enrich your Church with their children).
Lord, may they both praise you when they are happy
  and turn to you in their sorrows.
May they be glad that you help them in their work
  and know that you are with them in their need.
May they pray to you in the community of the Church,
  and be your witnesses in the world.
May they reach old age in the company of their friends,
  and come at last to the kingdom of heaven.
We ask this through Christ our Lord.   (Roman Catholic)

10.8

Almighty God, in whom we live and move and have our being,
  look graciously upon the world which you have made
  and for which your Son gave his life,

and especially on all
whom you make to be one flesh in holy marriage.
May their lives together
  be a sacrament [sign] of your love to this broken world,
  so that unity may overcome estrangement,
    forgiveness heal guilt, and joy overcome despair.
Lord, in your mercy, **Hear our prayer**.

May *Name* and *Name* so live together
    that the strength of their love
  may enrich our common life
    and become a sign of your faithfulness.
Lord, in your Mercy, **Hear our prayer**.

May they receive the gift and heritage of children
  and the grace to bring them up to know and love you.
Lord, in your mercy, **Hear our prayer**.

May their home be a place of truth, security, and love;
  and their lives an example of concern for others.
Lord, in your mercy, **Hear our prayer**.

May those who have witnessed these vows
  find their lives strengthened
  and their loyalties confirmed.
Lord, in your mercy, **Hear our prayer**.   (Canadian Anglican)

❧ 11. EXCHANGE OF VOWS

This is the heart of the wedding service, when the man and woman declare publicly their commitment to one another. The couple should make sure that the vows made between them accurately reflect their own beliefs and values. In many services, this is the one place where couples make their own individual changes. The woman and man face each other, joining hands, and speak to one another. The pastor may prompt them, line by line.

11.1

In the name of God,
I, *Name,* take you, *Name,* to be my wife/husband,
   to have and to hold
   from this day forward,
   for better, for worse,
   for richer, for poorer,
   in sickness and in health,
   to love and to cherish,
   until we are parted by death.
This is my solemn vow.   (United Methodist and Episcopalian)

11.2

I take you, *Name,* to be my wife/husband,
   and I promise before God and all who are present here
     to be your loving and faithful husband/wife
     as long as we both shall live.

I will serve you with tenderness and respect,
and encourage you to develop God's gifts in you.

(United Methodist)

11.3

Name, in the name of God,
   I take you to be my husband/wife from this time onward,
   to join with you and to share all that is to come,
   to give and to receive,
   to speak and to listen,
   to inspire and to respond,
   and in all our life together
   to be loyal to you with my whole being,
   as long as we both shall live.   (United Methodist)

11.4

I, *Name,* take you, *Name,*
   to be my wedded wife/husband,
   to have and to hold,
   from this day forward,
   for better, for worse,
   for richer, for poorer,
   in sickness and in health,
   to love and to cherish,
   till death us do part,
   according to God's holy ordinance;
   and thereto I pledge you my faith.   (Methodist)

11.5

I take you, *Name,*
   to be my wife/husband from this day forward,
   to join with you and share all that is to come,

and I promise to be faithful to you
until death parts us.   (Lutheran)

11.6

Name, I give myself to you to be your wife/husband.
I promise to love and sustain you in the covenant of marriage,
   from this day forward,
   in sickness and in health,
   in plenty and in want,
   in joy and in sorrow,
as long as we both shall live.   (United Church of Christ)

11.7

I, *Name,* take you *Name,* to be my wife/husband;
   and I promise,
before God and these witnesses,
   to be your loving and faithful husband/wife;
in plenty and in want;
in joy and in sorrow;
in sickness and in health;
as long as we both shall live.   (Presbyterian)

11.8

Before God and these witnesses,
   I, *Name*, take you, *Name,* to be my wife/husband,
and I promise to love you,
and to be faithful to you,
as long as we both shall live.   (Presbyterian)

11.9

I, *Name,* take you, *Name,* to be my wife/husband,
   according to God's holy will.

I will love you,
   and share my life with you,
in sickness and in health,
in poverty and in prosperity,
in conflict and in harmony,
as long as we both shall live.
This is my solemn vow.   (Australian)

11.10

I, *Name,* in the presence of God,
   take you, *Name,* to be my wife/husband.
All that I am I give to you,
   and all that I have I share with you.
Whatever the future holds,
   I will love you and stand by you,
as long as we both shall live.
This is my solemn vow.   (Australian)

11.11

Man to woman:

I, *Name,* take thee *Name,*
   to be my wife in Christian marriage.
I promise God,
   and I promise you
   that I will be Christian in my actions and attitudes.
I will serve the Lord with you;
   I will provide Christian leadership in our home.
I will work to meet our financial responsibilities;
   I will be faithful to you and to you alone.
I will weep with you in sorrow,

rejoice with you in blessings,
    and be your faithful companion until Christ calls us home.
I make this vow to you, so help me God.

Woman to man:

I, *Name,* take thee *Name,*
    to be my husband in the Lord.
I promise God, and I promise you that I will cherish you,
    I will obey you, I will love you,
    I will provide a shoulder to cry on,
        a heart that understands,
    a warm home for you to live in,
    and open arms for you to lean on.
I will pray for you and encourage you;
    I will weep when you weep,
    laugh when you laugh,
    and be yours and yours alone
        until our Lord separates us by death.
This I solemnly and joyfully promise,
    so help me God.   (Baptist)

11.12

I take you, as a gift from God,
    to be my lifelong companion
    through tears and laughter,
    sickness and health,
    work and play.
I will love you faithfully,
    constantly and prayerfully,
now and forever. **Amen**.   (Alternatives)

11.13

I promise to be faithful to you,
  open and honest with you.
I will respect, trust, help and care for you.
I will share my life with you.
I will forgive you as we have been forgiven.
I will lead with you a simple, just and peaceful life
  as Christ has called us to live.
And with you I will work to further simplicity, justice,
  and peace in our world.
I will love you
  and be thankful for the blessing of your love
  until death parts us.   (Alternatives)

11.14

Name, I commit myself to be with you
  in joy and adversity,
  in wholeness and brokenness,
  in peace and trouble,
  living with you in fidelity and love all our days.
                    (United Church of Canada)

11.15

Name, I give myself to you in marriage
  and vow to be your husband/wife
  all the days of our lives.
I give you my hands
  and take your hands in mine
    as a symbol and pledge
  of our uniting in one flesh.
I give you my love,

    the outpouring of my heart,
    as a symbol and pledge
    of our uniting in one spirit.
I give you this ring
    from out of my worldly goods
    as a symbol and pledge
      of our uniting as one family.   (Reformed Church)

11.16

I take you, *Name,* to be my wife/husband from this day forward,
    to join with you and share all that is to come,
      and with the help of God
I promise to be faithful to you as God gives us life together.
           (Evangelical Covenant)

🌿 12. TAKING, BLESSING, AND EXCHANGING OF RINGS

The wedding rings serve as a public witness that the man and woman are married. Other tangible symbols may be given in addition to, or instead of, rings. For example, these may include a loop of rosary beads (a Mexican tradition), or sips of sake (a Japanese tradition), or the giving of a mangalasutra (Church of South India). It was traditional for the man only to give a ring to the woman, but today, most services include both the man and the woman giving and receiving rings. Be sure that the words at the Taking, Blessing, and Exchanging of Rings complement one another.

The pastor, taking the rings, says one of the following:

12a.1

These rings (symbols)
are the outward and visible sign
   of an inward and spiritual grace,
signifying to us the union
   between Jesus Christ and his Church.   (United Methodist)

12a.2

These rings (symbols)
are the outward and visible sign

    of an inward and spiritual grace,
    signifying to all the uniting of *Name* and *Name*
      in holy marriage.   (United Methodist)

12a.3

The wedding ring is the outward and visible sign
    of an inward and spiritual grace,
signifying to all the uniting
    of this man and woman in holy matrimony,
through the Church of Jesus Christ our Lord.   (Methodist)

The pastor may then bless the giving of rings or other symbols of the marriage:

12b.1

Bless, O Lord, the giving of these rings (symbols),
that they who wear them may live in your peace
    and continue in your favor
    all the days of their life;
through Jesus Christ our Lord. **Amen.**   (United Methodist)

12b.2

Bless, O Lord, the giving of these rings,
that they who wear them may abide in thy peace,
    and continue in thy favor;
through Jesus Christ our Lord. **Amen.**   (Methodist)

12b.3

Bless, O Lord, this ring to be a sign of the vows
    by which this man and this woman
    have bound themselves to each other;
through Jesus Christ our Lord. **Amen.**   (Episcopalian)

12b.4

By these symbols of covenant promise, Gracious God,
  remind *Name* and *Name*
  of your encircling love and unending faithfulness
    that in all their life together
  they may know joy and peace in one another. **Amen.**

(United Church of Christ)

12b.5

Eternal God,
  who in the time of Noah
  gave us the rainbow as a sign of promise,
  bless these symbols that they also may be signs of promises
    fulfilled in lives of faithful loving;
through Jesus Christ our Savior. **Amen.**

(United Church of Christ)

12b.6

By your blessing, O God,
  may these rings be to *Name* and *Name*
    symbols of unending love and faithfulness,
reminding them of the covenant they have made this day,
through Jesus Christ our Lord. **Amen.**   (Presbyterian)

12b.7

Bless O Lord these rings.
Bless him/her who gives and bless her/him who wears,
    and bless her/him who gives and him/her who wears,
    that they may live together in love and harmony,
through Jesus Christ our Savior. **Amen.**

(African Methodist Episcopal)

12b.8

Blessed are you, God of steadfast love,
  source of our joy and end of our hope.
Bless this ring [these rings] given and received
  that it [they] may be a symbol of the vow and covenant
Name and *Name* have made this day,
  through Jesus Christ our Lord. **Amen.**   (Canadian Anglican)

While placing the ring on the third finger of the recipient's left hand, the giver may say prompted, line by line, by the pastor:

12c.1

Name, I give you this ring
  as a sign of my vow,
and with all that I am,
    and all that I have, I honor you;
in the name of the Father,
  and of the Son, and of the Holy Spirit
(or in the Name of God).   (Episcopalian and United Methodist)

12c.2

In token and pledge
  of our constant faith and abiding love,
with this ring I thee wed,
in the name of the Father,
  and of the Son,
    and of the Holy Spirit. **Amen.**   (Methodist)

12c.3

I give you this ring as a sign of my love and faithfulness.

(Lutheran)

12c.4

Name, I give you this symbol
  as a sign of my love and faithfulness.

Response:

Name, I receive this symbol
  as a sign of our love and faithfulness.

(United Church of Christ)

12c.5

Name, I give you this ring as a sign of our covenant,
  in the name of the Father,
  and of the Son,
  and of the Holy Spirit. **Amen.**

Response:

I receive this ring as a sign of our covenant,
  in the name of the Father,
  and of the Son,
  and of the Holy Spirit. **Amen.**   (Presbyterian)

12c.6

In all ages and among all peoples,
  the ring has been a symbol of that which is measureless,
    a symbol of measureless, boundless devotion.
It is a circle;
  it has neither beginning nor ending.
A circle of precious gold,
  indicating the longevity of your love
and the pricelessness of your devotion.   (Baptist, altered)

12c.7

With this ring I wed you,
 and I endow you with my worldly possession,
in the name of the Father, and of the Son, and of the
Holy Ghost. **Amen.**   (African Methodist Episcopal)

❦ 13. UNITY CANDLE

The unity candle is a recent addition to the wedding service, another visible sign that the husband and wife have become one.

If a unity candle is used, the two side candles representing the husband and wife are lighted first, often by the respective mothers or other members of the family, while the family is being seated at the beginning of the service.

The center candle representing the marriage is lighted after the giving of the rings or at some later point in the service. The side candles are not extinguished because both husband and wife retain their personal identities.

During the lighting of the unity candle, music may be played or sung.

During the lighting, it often seems best if no words are spoken, so that the congregation may focus on the symbolic action of the lighting of the unity candle. Or someone may read one of the following:

13.1

The ancient candle ceremony symbolizes
   the one-flesh principle in Christian marriage.
The two become one and treat each other
   as if they were a part of their own flesh.
The love that comes out of this unity is best described
   by Ruth's words to Naomi in the Old Testament:
"Do not press me to leave you
   or to turn back from following you!
Where you go, I will go;

where you lodge, I will lodge; your people shall be my people,
and your God my God.
Where you die, I will die —
there will I be buried." Ruth 1:16-17
In Christ the two become one. (Baptist)

13.2

Name and *Name* light the unity candle,
symbolizing that in marriage they are no longer two people,
but in Christ they become one flesh. (Baptist)

13.3

Then the man said:
"This at last is bone of my bones
and flesh of my flesh;
this one shall be called woman,
for out of man this one was taken."
Therefore a man leaves his father and his mother
and clings to his wife,
and they become one flesh. Genesis 2:23-24

❧ 14. DECLARATION OF MARRIAGE

The pastor now declares to the congregation that the couple are now husband and wife. The wife and husband join hands, and the pastor may place a hand on their joined hands. Or, as the couple joins hands, the pastor may wrap a stole around their joined hands, as a sign of their union.

14.1

Pastor to couple:

You have declared your consent and vows
  before God and this congregation.
May God confirm your covenant
  and fill you both with grace.

Pastor to people:

Now that *Name* and *Name*
  have given themselves to each other by solemn vows,
  with the joining of hands,
  [and the giving and receiving of rings,]

I pronounce (announce to you) that they are husband and wife;
  in the name of the Father,
  and of the Son, and of the Holy Spirit.

Those whom God has joined together,
  let no one put asunder. **Amen.**

(United Methodist and Episcopalian)

14.2

Forasmuch as *Name* and *Name* have consented together
    in holy wedlock,
  and have witnessed the same before God and this company,
    and thereto have pledged their faith each to the other,
  and have declared the same
    by joining hands and by giving and receiving rings;
I pronounce that they are husband and wife together,
  in the name of the Father,
  and of the Son,
  and of the Holy Spirit.
Those whom God hath joined together,
  let no one put asunder. **Amen.**   (Methodist)

14.3

Name and *Name*,
  by their promises before God
  and in the presence of this congregation,
have bound themselves to one another as husband and wife.
**Blessed be the Father and the Son and the Holy Spirit
  now and forever.**
Those whom God has joined together let no one put asunder.
Amen.   (Lutheran)

14.4

Pastor to couple:

Name and *Name,*
>
> you have committed yourselves to each other
> in this joyous and sacred covenant.

Become one. Fulfill your promises.
Love and serve God, honor Christ and each other,
> and rejoice in the power of the Holy Spirit.

Pastor to congregation:

By their promises, made before us this day, *Name* and *Name*
> have united themselves as husband and wife
> in sacred covenant.

Those whom God has joined together let no one separate.

(United Church of Christ)

14.5

Name and *Name,* you are husband and wife
> with the blessing of Christ's church.

Be merciful in all your ways, kind in heart,
> and humble in mind.

Accept life, and be most patient and tolerant with one another.
Forgive as freely as God has forgiven you.
And, above everything else, be truly loving.
Let the peace of Christ rule in your hearts,
> remembering that as members of one body
> you are called to live in harmony,

and never forget to be thankful for what God has done for you.

(United Church of Christ)

14.6

Hear the words of our Lord Jesus Christ:
> From the beginning of creation,
> God made them male and female.

CHRISTIAN WEDDINGS

For this reason a man shall leave his father and mother
 and be joined to his wife, and the two shall become one.
So they are no longer two but one.
Let no one separate those whom God has joined together.

(Australian)

Following the Declaration of Marriage, the congregation may be invited to stand, and a doxology or hymn may be sung, as a sign of celebration and response to the marriage. The following hymns are suggested:

Praise to the Lord, the Almighty
The Gift of Love
When Love Is Found

15. BLESSING OF THE MARRIAGE

The pastor prays for the couple and offers the church's blessing to the marriage. The husband and wife may kneel, or remain standing, as the pastor prays.

15.1

O God,
you have so consecrated the covenant of Christian marriage
that in it is represented
the covenant between Christ and his Church.
Send therefore your blessing upon *Name* and *Name*,
that they may surely keep their marriage covenant,
and so grow in love and godliness together
that their home may be a haven of blessing and peace;
through Jesus Christ our Lord. **Amen.**

(Episcopalian and United Methodist)

15.2

Most gracious God,
we give you thanks for your tender love
in making us a covenant people
through our Savior Jesus Christ
and for consecrating in his name
the marriage covenant of *Name* and *Name*.
Grant that their love for each other
may reflect the love of Christ for us

and grow from strength to strength
as they faithfully serve you in the world.
Defend them from every enemy.
Lead them into all peace.
Let their love for each other
be a seal upon their hearts,
a mantle about their shoulders,
and a crown upon their heads.
Bless them in their work and in their companionship;
in their sleeping and in their waking;
in their joys and in their sorrows;
in their lives and in their deaths.
Finally, by your grace,
bring them and all of us to that table
where your saints feast for ever
in your heavenly home;
through Jesus Christ our Lord,
who with you and the Holy Spirit
lives and reigns,
one God, for ever and ever. **Amen.**

(United Methodist and Episcopalian)

15.3

O eternal God,
creator and preserver of us all,
giver of all spiritual grace,
the author of everlasting life:
Send thy blessing upon *Name* and *Name,*
whom we bless in thy name;
that they may surely perform and keep
the vow and covenant between them made,

and may ever remain in perfect love and peace together
    and live according to thy laws.
Look graciously upon them,
    that they may love, honor, and cherish each other,
    and so live together in faithfulness and patience,
        in wisdom and true godliness,
    that their home may be a haven of blessing
        and a place of peace;
through Jesus Christ our Lord. **Amen.**   (Methodist)

15.4

The Lord God,
    who created our first parents
    and established them in marriage,
establish and sustain you,
    that you may find delight in each other
and grow in holy love until your life's end. **Amen**.   (Lutheran)

15.5

Let us bless God for all the gifts in which we rejoice today.
Lord God, constant in mercy, great in faithfulness:
With high praise we recall
    your acts of unfailing love
    for the human family,
    for the house of Israel, and for your people the Church.
We bless you for the joy which your servants, *Name* and *Name,*
    have found in each other,
and pray that you give to us such a sense of your constant love
    that we may employ all our strength
    in a life of praise of you,
whose work alone holds true and endures forever. **Amen.**
                        (Lutheran)

15.6

Let us pray for *Name* and *Name* in their life together.
Faithful Lord, source of love,
   pour down your grace upon *Name* and *Name*,
that they may fulfill the vows they have made this day,
   and reflect your steadfast love
   in their life-long faithfulness to each other.
As members with them of the body of Christ,
   use us to support their life together;
and from your great store of strength
   give them power and patience,
   affection and understanding, courage and love
toward you, toward each other, and toward the world,
that they may continue together in mutual growth
according to your will in Jesus Christ our Lord. **Amen.**

(Lutheran)

15.7

The grace of Christ attend you;
   the love of God surround you;
   the Holy Spirit keep you that may grow in holy love,
     find delight in each other always,
   and remain faithful until your life's end. **Amen.**

(United Church of Christ)

15.8

May the God of Sarah and Abraham,
   who watches over all the families of the earth,
   bless your new family
   and establish your home in peace and steadfast love.
Amen.
(United Church of Christ)

15.9

Merciful God, we thank you for your love that lives within us
   and calls us from loneliness to companionship.
We thank you for all who have gone before us:
   for Adam and Eve, for Sarah and Abraham,
   for Joseph and Mary,
   and for countless parents whose names we do not know.
We thank you for our own parents,
   and for all, whether married or single,
   who are mother or father to us,
   as we grow to the fullness of the stature of Christ.
Bless *Name* and *Name*,
   that they may have the grace
   to live the promises they have made.
Defend them from all enemies of their love.
Teach them the patience of undeserved forgiveness.
Bring them to old age,
   rejoicing in love's winter more fully than in its springtime.
Amen.   (United Church of Christ)

15.10

Pastor for children of new marriage:

Bless this child/these children,
   that he/she/they may find in this new home
   a haven of love and joy
where Jesus Christ is honored in kind words and tender deeds.
                                          (United Church of Christ)

15.11

Blessed are you, heavenly Father:
  You give joy to bridegroom and bride.
Blessed are you, Lord Jesus Christ:
  You have brought new life to the world.
Blessed are you, Holy Spirit of God:
  You bring us together in love.
Blessed be Father, Son and Holy Spirit:
  One God to be praised for ever. Amen.   (Australian)

15.12

The pastor may pray the following:

In peace, let us pray to the Lord:
All grace comes from you, O God,
  and you alone are the source of eternal life.
Bless your servants *Name* and *Name,*
  that they may faithfully live together to the end of their lives.
May they be patient and gentle, ready to trust each other,
  and to face together the challenge of the future.
May they pray together in joy and in sorrow,
  and always give thanks for the gift of each other.
Be with them in all their happiness;
  that your joy may be in them, and their joy may be full.
Strengthen them in every time of trouble,
  that they may bear each other's burdens,
  and so fulfil the law of Christ.
Give *Name* and *Name* grace, when they hurt each other,
  to recognize and acknowledge their fault,
  to ask each other's forgiveness,
  and to know your mercy and love.

May your peace dwell in their home,
   and be a sign of hope for peace in the world.
Let their home be a place of welcome,
   that its happiness may be freely shared.
Through loving one another in Christ,
   may they be strengthened to love Christ in their neighbor.
May they be creative in their daily work,
   and find fulfillment in the life of their community.

(The following two prayers may be included:)

May *Name* and *Name* enjoy the gift and heritage of children.
Grant that they may be loving and wise parents,
   with grace to bring up their children
   to know you, to love you and to serve you.

or

May *Name* and *Name*
   enjoy the gift and heritage of their children.
Grant them the grace to share their love and faith
   with *Names of Children*
that they may grow together as a loving family.

Bless the parents and families of *Name* and *Name,*
   that they may be united in love and friendship.
Grant that all married people
   who have witnessed these vows today
   may find their lives strengthened
   and their loyalties confirmed.
We ask these prayers in the name of Christ our Lord. **Amen.**
                                                            (Australian)

15.13

Pastor for all families:

Gracious Father, you bless family life and renew your people.
Enrich husbands and wives, parents and children
  more and more with your grace,
  that, strengthening and supporting each other,
  they may serve those in need
  and be a sign of the fulfillment of your kingdom,
where, with your Son Jesus Christ and the Holy Spirit,
you live and reign, one God through all ages. **Amen.**

(Australian)

15.14

Almighty and most merciful God,
  who has now united this man and this woman
    in the holy estate of matrimony,
  grant them grace to live therein
    according to your holy word.
Strengthen them in constant fidelity
    and true affection toward each other;
  sustain and defend them amid all the trials and temptations,
    and help them so to pass through this world
    in faith toward you,
  in communion with your holy church,
    and in loving service one of the other
  that they may enjoy forever your heavenly benediction,
through Jesus Christ, your Son, our Lord,
who lives and reigns with you and the Holy Ghost,
ever One God, world without end. **Amen.**

(African Methodist Episcopal)

15.15

Almighty God,
  you send your Holy Spirit
    to be the life and light of all your people.
Open the hearts of these your children to the riches of his grace,
  that they may bring forth the fruit of the Spirit
    in love and joy and peace
through Jesus Christ our Lord. **Amen.**   (Church of England)

15.16

Heavenly Father, maker of all things,
  you enable us to share in your work of creation.
Bless this couple in the gift and care of children,
  that their home may be a place of love, security, and truth,
    and their children grow up
    to know and love you in your Son
    Jesus Christ our Lord. **Amen.**   (Church of England)

15.17

Lord and Savior Jesus Christ,
  who shared at Nazareth the life of an earthly home:
  reign in the home of these your servants as Lord and King;
  give them grace to minister to others
    as you have ministered to them,
  and grant that by deed and word
    they may be witnesses of your saving love
  to those among whom they live;
  for the sake of your holy name. **Amen.** (Church of England)

15.18

All grace comes from you, O God,
  and you alone are the source of eternal life.

Bless your servants *Name* and *Name*,
  that they may faithfully live together
    to the end of their lives.
Be with them in all their happiness
  that your joy may be in them,
    and their joy may be full.
Strengthen them in every time of trouble
  that they may carry each other's burdens
    and so fulfill the law of Christ.
Let your blessing be on their home
  that your peace may dwell there.
Let it be a place of welcome
  that its happiness may be freely shared.
Bless the families and friends of *Name* and *Name*
  that we may be united in love and friendship.
Now to him who is able to keep you from falling
  and to present you faultless
  before the presence of his glory with rejoicing,
    to the only God, our Savior, through Jesus Christ our Lord,
be glory, majesty, dominion and authority,
both now and for ever. **Amen**.   (British Methodist)

15.19

May there be truth and understanding between you.
May you enjoy length of days,
  fulfillment of hopes, and peace and contentment of mind.
May God bless and keep you always.

                                          (United Church of Canada)

15.20

Most merciful and gracious God,
  we thank you for the love

with which you bind human souls together,
and especially for the covenant of marriage,
the tenderness of its ties,
the honor of its estate,
and the sacredness of its obligations.
Look with favor upon your servants, *Name* and *Name*,
sanctify and bless their union;
grant them grace to fulfill, with pure and steadfast affection,
the vow and covenant made between them.
Guide them together, we pray,
in the way of righteousness and peace,
that, loving and serving you,
all the days of their life,
they may be abundantly enriched by your grace.
Grant them the guidance of the Holy Spirit,
and teach them to do all that
which is well pleasing in your sight,
through Jesus Christ, our Lord. **Amen**.   (Moravian)

15.21

O God, you have so consecrated the covenant of marriage
that in it is represented the spiritual unity
between Christ and his Church;
Send therefore your blessing upon these your servants,
that they may so love, honor, and cherish each other
in faithfulness and patience, in wisdom and true godliness,
that their home may be a haven of blessing and peace;
through Jesus Christ our Lord,
who lives and reigns with you and the Holy Spirit,
one God, now and for ever. **Amen**.   (Episcopalian)

*At the end of the prayer, the pastor invites the congregation to
pray* The Lord's Prayer (next chapter).

*A Filipino tradition directs the couple to feed one another cooked
rice at this time, while at an Armenian wedding two white doves
are released as signs of love and happiness. A traditional Greek
wedding would here include placing crowns of orange blossoms
(signs of purity and loveliness) on the heads of the couple.*

16. THE LORD'S PRAYER

The Lord's Prayer, the prayer Jesus taught his disciples to pray, is prayed by everyone, using one of the forms below. The wife and husband may continue to kneel (traditional) or may stand. Or the Lord's Prayer may be sung by a soloist or as a hymn by the congregation. Or the prayer may be prayed following the Prayer of Thanksgiving, if Holy Communion is served.

16.1

ECUMENICAL TEXT

Our Father in heaven, hallowed be your name,
your kingdom come, your will be done, on earth as in heaven.
Give us today our daily bread.
Forgive us our sins as we forgive those who sin against us.
Save us from the time of trial and deliver us from evil.
For the kingdom, the power, and the glory are yours
now and forever. **Amen.**

16.2

TRADITIONAL TEXT #1

Our Father, who art in heaven, hallowed be thy name.
Thy kingdom come, thy will be done, on earth as it is in heaven.
Give us this day our daily bread.
And forgive us our trespasses
as we forgive those who trespass against us.

And lead us not into temptation, but deliver us from evil.
For thine is the kingdom, and the power, and the glory,
    forever. **Amen.**

16.3
TRADITIONAL TEXT #2

Our Father, who art in heaven, hallowed be thy name;
    thy kingdom come, thy will be done, on earth as it is in heaven.
Give us this day our daily bread;
and forgive us our debts
    as we forgive our debtors;
and lead us not into temptation, but deliver us from evil.
For thine is the kingdom and the power and the glory,
    forever. **Amen.**

🍃 17. THANKSGIVING AND COMMUNION

Holy Communion may be celebrated as the first act of the married couple. Such a action is not a mournful or somber ritual but a celebrative moment recognizing God's love. If communion is a part of the service, it is most important that the service is included in a service that includes the reading of Scripture. Also, not only the husband and wife but the whole congregation should be invited to receive communion. It is the United Methodist and United Church of Christ tradition, among others, to invite all Christians to the Lord's table, but other traditions may limit who may receive (for example, non-Roman Catholics may not receive at a Roman Catholic service where a priest presides). Finally, there should be no pressure that would embarrass those who for whatever reason do not choose to receive communion.

The husband and wife, or children from previous marriages, or representatives of the congregation may bring bread and wine/cup to the Lord's table.

The pastor, standing if possible behind the Lord's table, facing the people from this time through Breaking the Bread, takes the bread and cup; and the bread and wine are prepared for the meal.

The bread and wine are given first to the couple and then to the people, and the husband and wife may assist in the distribution.

While the bread and cup are given, the congregation may sing hymns, or there may be vocal or instrumental music.

The pastor will probably choose the appropriate prayer at the table, according to each church's own tradition. The following are two examples of prayers at the table.

THE GREAT THANKSGIVING

17.1

The Lord be with you.
And also with you.
Lift up your hearts.
We lift them up to the Lord.
Let us give thanks to the Lord our God.
It is right to give our thanks and praise.

It is right, and a good and joyful thing,
    always and everywhere to give thanks to you,
    Father Almighty (almighty God),
    Creator of heaven and earth.
You formed us in your image, male and female you created us.
You gave us the gift of marriage,
    that we might fulfill each other.
And so,
    with your people on earth and all the company of heaven
    we praise your Name and join their unending hymn:

Holy, holy, holy Lord, God of power and might,
heaven and earth are full of your glory.
    Hosanna in the highest.
Blessed is he who comes in the Name of the Lord.
    Hosanna in the highest.

Holy are you, and blessed is your Son Jesus Christ.
By the baptism of his suffering, death, and resurrection
    you gave birth to your Church,
    delivered us from slavery to sin and death,

and made with us a new covenant
by water and the Spirit,
   from which flows the covenant love of husband and wife.
On the night in which he gave himself up for us,
   he took bread, gave thanks to you, broke the bread,
   gave it to his disciples, and said:
"Take, eat; this is my body which is given for you.
Do this in remembrance of me."
When the supper was over he took the cup,
   gave thanks to you, gave it to his disciples, and said:
"Drink from this, all of you;
   this is my blood of the new covenant,
   poured out for you and for many
      for the forgiveness of sins.
Do this, as often as you drink it,
   in remembrance of me."
And so,
in remembrance of these your mighty acts in Jesus Christ,
we offer ourselves in praise and thanksgiving
   as a holy and living sacrifice,
   in union with Christ's offering for us,
as we proclaim the mystery of faith:

Christ has died; Christ is risen; Christ will come again.

Pour out your Holy Spirit on us gathered here,
   and on these gifts of bread and wine.
Make them be for us the body and blood of Christ,
that we may be for the world the body of Christ,
   redeemed by his blood.
By the same bless *Name* and *Name,*

that their love for each other
    may reflect the love of Christ for us
    and grow from strength to strength
as they faithfully serve you in the world.
Defend them from every enemy.
Lead them into all peace.
Let their love for each other
    be a seal upon their hearts,
    a mantle about their shoulders,
    and a crown upon their heads.
Bless them
    in their work and in their companionship;
    in their sleeping and in their waking;
    in their joys and in their sorrows;
    in their lives and in their deaths.
Finally, by your grace,
bring them and all of us to that table
    where your saints feast for ever in your heavenly home.
Through your Son Jesus Christ,
with the Holy Spirit in your holy Church,
all honor and glory is yours, almighty Father (God),
now and for ever. **Amen.**   (United Methodist)

17.2

The Lord be with you.
And also with you.
Lift up your hearts.
We lift them up to the Lord.
Let us give thanks to the Lord our God.
It is right to give our thanks and praise.

Blessed are you, O God our Creator.

From the womb of your being you brought forth worlds.
Into mere dust you blew the breath of life,
   creating women and men to bear your likeness in the world.
You create, love, and care for all that is.
We praise you and thank you, nurturing God,
   that in Jesus you bring joy and hope to loving hearts,
   and offer health and power to human relationships.
Even the powers of sorrow and death
   could not contain Christ's joy.
From the tomb our risen Savior came
   to share bread again among the beloved.
In the glory of your banquet hall,
Christ prepares a wedding feast
   for all the faithful who even now praise you.

Holy, holy, holy, God of love and majesty,
the whole universe speaks of your glory,
   O God Most High.
Blessed is the one who comes in the name of the our God!
   Hosanna in the highest!

Merciful God,
   we remember that on the night of betrayal and desertion,
   Jesus took bread, gave thanks to you, broke the bread,
     and gave it to the disciples saying:
"Take, eat; this is my body broken for you.
Likewise, Jesus took the cup of blessing and said:
"Drink of this cup. It is the new covenant in my blood,
   poured out for you and for many for the forgiveness of sins.
Do this in memory of me."
With joy we thank you, God of gladness and warmth,

that at Pentecost you sent your Holy Spirit
    to dance about the heads of your people,
enabling your word to be heard afresh.
Now send your Holy Spirit
    on these gifts of bread and wine on us
    that we may be set afire with your love
    and leap with joy at your presence.
Pour out your blessing on *Name* and *Name*.
May they sing a new song of your great love
    in communion with you
    and all your saints in heaven and on earth.
May their love for each other
    proclaim the love of Christ for all of us.
May the faithful service of all your people
    bring peace, justice, joy, and love to all the world;
through Christ, with Christ, and in Christ,
in the unity of the Holy Spirit,
all glory and honor are your, Holy God, now and forever.
Amen.   (United Church of Christ)

The Lord's Prayer may then be prayed (see Chapter 16).
All receive the bread and cup, beginning with the couple.
When all have received, the Lord's table is put in order.

The pastor may offer one of the following prayers after
communion:

17.3

Eternal God, we give you thanks
that you have brought *Name* and *Name*
[and their families and friends]

together at the table of your family.
Help them grow in love and unity,
that they may rejoice together all the days of their lives
  and in the wedding feast of heaven.
Grant this through Jesus Christ our Lord. **Amen.**

(United Methodist)

17.4

O God, the giver of all that is true and lovely and gracious;
We give you thanks for binding us together
  in these holy mysteries
  of the Body and Blood of your Son Jesus Christ.
Grant that by your Holy Spirit, *Name* and *Name,*
  now joined in Holy Matrimony,
  may become one in heart and soul, live in fidelity and peace,
and obtain those eternal joys prepared for all who love you;
for the sake of Jesus Christ our Lord. **Amen.**   (Episcopalian)

17.5

Thank you, O God, for refreshing us at your table.
By your grace you have nourished us
  with the living presence of Christ, the bread of life,
    that we may share life together.
Send us forth in the power of your Holy Spirit
  to give ourselves in love
  until your entire human family is gathered at your table,
glorifying and praising you in the Name of Jesus Christ. **Amen.**

(United Church of Christ)

17.6

Loving God, we thank you that you have fed us in this holy meal,
    united us with Christ,
and given us a foretaste of the marriage feast of the Lamb.
So strengthen us in your service
    that our daily living may show our thanks,
through Jesus Christ our Lord. **Amen.**   (Presbyterian)

❧ 18. DISMISSAL WITH BLESSING

The service is almost over, and the pastor sends out the couple and congregation to serve God and one another. Here may be sung a hymn or psalm, before the pastor offers one of the following final blessings for the couple and the congregation.

18.1

Pastor to wife and husband:

God the Eternal keep you in love with each other,
   so that the peace of Christ may abide in your home.
Go to serve God and your neighbor in all that you do.

Pastor to people:

Bear witness to the love of God in this world,
   so that those to whom love is a stranger
     will find in you generous friends.
The grace of the Lord Jesus Christ,
   and the love of God,
   and the communion of the Holy Spirit
   be with you all. **Amen.**   (United Methodist)

18.2

God the Father, the Son, and the Holy Spirit
   bless, preserve, and keep you;

the Lord graciously with his favor look upon you,
and so fill you with all spiritual benediction and love
    that you may so live together in this life
    that in the world to come you may have life everlasting.
Amen.   (Methodist)

18.3

Almighty God, Father, Son, and Holy Spirit,
    keep you in his light and truth and love now and forever.
Amen.   (Lutheran)

18.4

Go forth in the love of God;
    go forth in hope and joy,
    knowing that God is with you always.
And the peace of God which passes all understanding,
    keep your hearts and minds
    in the knowledge and love of God and of Christ Jesus;
and the blessing of God, Creator, Redeemer, and Sanctifier,
be with you, and remain with you always. **Amen.**
                            (United Church of Christ)

18.5

May God bless you and keep you.
May God's face shine upon you and be gracious to you.
May God look upon you with kindness and give you peace.
Amen.   (United Church of Christ)

18.6

As God's own, clothe yourselves
with compassion, kindness, and patience,

forgiving each other as the Lord has forgiven you,
and crown all these things with love,
which binds everything together in perfect harmony.

(Presbyterian)

18.7

Whatever you do, in word or deed,
do everything in the name of the Lord Jesus,
giving thanks to God through him. (Presbyterian)

18.8

The grace of Christ attend you,
the love of God surrounding you,
the Holy Spirit keep you,
that you may live in faith, abound in hope, and grow in love,
both now and forevermore. **Amen.** (Presbyterian)

18.9

God the Father, God the Son, God the Holy Spirit, bless, preserve, and keep you;
the Lord mercifully with his favor look upon you, and fill you with all spiritual benediction and grace;
that you may faithfully live together in this life, and in the age to come have life everlasting. **Amen.**

(Episcopalian)

The couple may greet each other with a kiss and be greeted by the pastor, after which greetings may be exchanged throughout the congregation.

The pastor may introduce the couple to the congregation by saying one of the following:

18.10

It is my privilege to introduce to you Mr. and Mrs. John Smith *(groom's full name)*.

18.11

I introduce to you Mr. and Mrs. John Smith *(groom's full name)* and Jane Doe *(bride's full name)*.

18.12

I introduce to you Mr. and Mrs. John *(groom's first name)* and Jane *(bride's first name)* Smith.

A hymn may be sung or instrumental music played as the couple, the wedding party, and the people leave. The following recessional hymns are suggested:

All Praise to Thee, for Thou, O King Divine
Come We That Love the Lord
God, Whose Love Is Reigning o'er Us
Joyful, Joyful, We Adore Thee
Love Divine, All Loves Excelling
Now Thank We All Our God
Ye Watchers and Ye Holy Ones

ACKNOWLEDGMENTS

Every effort has been made to trace the owner(s) and/or administrator(s) of each copyright. The Publisher regrets any omission and will, upon written notice, make the necessary correction(s) in subsequent printings.

Scripture, unless otherwise indicated, is adapted from the New Revised Standard Version of the Bible, © 1989 by Division of Christian Education of the National Council of Churches of Christ in the USA and is used by permission.

African Methodist Episcopal; The A.M.E. Sunday School Union.

Alternatives; Margaret and Mark Yackel-Juleen and Donna Rose-Heim. Used with permission.

Australian; from *An Australian Prayer Book* © Anglican Church of Australia Trust Corporation. Reproduced with permission.

Baptist; from *The Wedding Collection* by Morris Chapman. © 1991 Broadman Press. All rights reserved. Used by permission.

British Methodist; © The Methodist Conference 1974. Used by permission of the Methodist Publishing House.

Canadian Anglican; from the Book of *Alternative Services* of the Anglican Church of Canada, published by the Anglican Book Centre 1985. Used with permission.

Church of England; with permission of the Central Board of Finance of the Church of England.

Church of Scotland; the Church of Scotland.

Church of South India; from the *Book of Common Worship of the Church of South India*, © Oxford University Press.

CHRISTIAN WEDDINGS

Episcopalian; although copyright permission is not required for use of items from *The Book of Common Prayer*, as a courtesy, we acknowledge this source.

Evangelical Covenant; © Covenant Publications, 1981.

Evangelical United Brethren; © 1992 United Methodist Publishing House, 201 8th Avenue S., Nashville, TN 37203.

Lutheran; reprinted from *Lutheran Book of Worship*, copyright © 1978, by permission of Augsburg Fortress.

Methodist; © 1992 United Methodist Publishing House, 201 8th Avenue S., Nashville, TN 37203.

Moravian; from *Moravian Book of Worship*, 1995. Used by permission.

Presbyterian; from *Book of Common Worship*. © 1993 Westminster/John Knox Press. Used by permission of Westminster/John Knox Press.

Reformed; *Liturgy and Psalms*, Gerrit T. Vander Lugt, editor. Copyright 1968 by the Board of Education of the Reformed Church in America. Used with permission.

Roman Catholic; excerpts from the English translation of *Rite of Marriage* © 1969, International Committee on English in the Liturgy, Inc. (ICEL); excerpts from the English translation of *The Roman Missal* © 1973, ICEL. All rights reserved.

United Church of Canada; used by permission of The United Church of Canada.

United Church of Christ; adapted from *Book of Worship United Church of Christ* © 1986 United Church of Christ, Office for Church Life and Leadership, New York. Used by permission.

United Methodist; *A Service of Christian Marriage I*. From *The United Methodist Book of Worship*. © 1992 United Methodist Publishing House. Used by permission.